KICKBOXING

BY THOMAS STREISSGUTH

D1364483

BELLWETHER MEDIA • MINNEAPOLIS, MN

Are you ready to take it to the extreme? Torque books thrust you into the action-packed world of sports, vehicles, and adventure. These books may include dirt, smoke, fire, and dangerous stunts.
WARNING: Read at your own risk.

This edition first published in 2008 by Bellwether Media.

No part of this publication may be reproduced in whole or in part without written permission of the publisher. For information regarding permission, write to Bellwether Media Inc., Attention: Permissions Department, Post Office Box 19349, Minneapolis, MN 55419

Library of Congress Cataloging-in-Publication Data

Streissguth, Thomas, 1958-
  Kickboxing / by Thomas Streissguth.
    p. cm. -- (Torque: Action sports)
  Summary: "Amazing photography accompanies engaging information about Kickboxing. The combination of high-interest subject matter and light text is intended for students in grades 3 through 7"--Provided by publisher.
  Includes bibliographical references and index.
  ISBN-13: 978-1-60014-140-9 (hardcover : alk. paper)
  ISBN-10: 1-60014-140-4 (hardcover : alk. paper)
  1. Kickboxing--Juvenile literature. I. Title.

  GV1114.65.S77 2008
  796.815--dc22
                                                        2007040751

CONTENTS

WHAT IS KICKBOXING?

Kickboxing is fast, furious, and physical. Kickboxers punch, kick, duck, and spin. They stay on their toes and move constantly. Some people practice kickboxing for fitness. No one fights back during practice.

Other people fight against **opponents**. The goal in that case is to use strength, skills, and **stamina** to physically overpower an opponent. Most kickboxers compete as amateurs. A few become professionals.

Matt Skelton
*World Kickboxing
Association Champ*

faSt faCt

Kickboxing is the national sport in Thailand. The most popular form of it is called Muay Thai, or "The Art of the Eight Limbs."

Competitive kickboxing is a kind of **martial art**. Some people describe it as a "full contact" sport. In other martial arts such as traditional **karate**, fighters control their moves in order to limit body contact. In kickboxing, contact between fighters is a key part of the sport.

Imogen Shayler
British World Champ

RULES AND EQUIPMENT

Kickboxing has different forms in different places. Rules are different depending on the form. In the United States, most people practice a form that bans punches and kicks below the waist. Fighters cannot strike with elbows and knees. They also must use at least eight kicks in each **round** of fighting.

10.oz

BOXN

Kickboxing requires very little equipment, no matter which form is practiced. Most fighters wear boxing gloves and mouthpieces. Loose trunks let fighters move easily. Most fighters go barefoot.

Fighters under age 18 always wear **headgear** made of leather or foam. This helps prevent injuries that could be caused by a punch or kick to the head. Adult fighters often use headgear in training but not in competition. They must rely on defensive moves to prevent direct hits to the head.

One of the most famous moves in Thai kickboxing is "throwing buffalo." The throwing buffalo move will knock out a water buffalo in one blow.

KICKBOXING
IN ACTION

Kickboxers train hard for competitions. They may practice with a punching bag or **spar** with another fighter. Sparring is practicing moves against a partner without using full force. Fighters can work on reactions and defense without the risk of getting hurt.

A kickboxing match may have as many as 12 rounds. Each round lasts two or three minutes. The fighters get one minute of rest between rounds. Judges award points for solid blows. Fighters also win points by forcing opponents to the ground. A match can end with a **knockout** or **surrender**. Points decide the winner if neither of those happens.

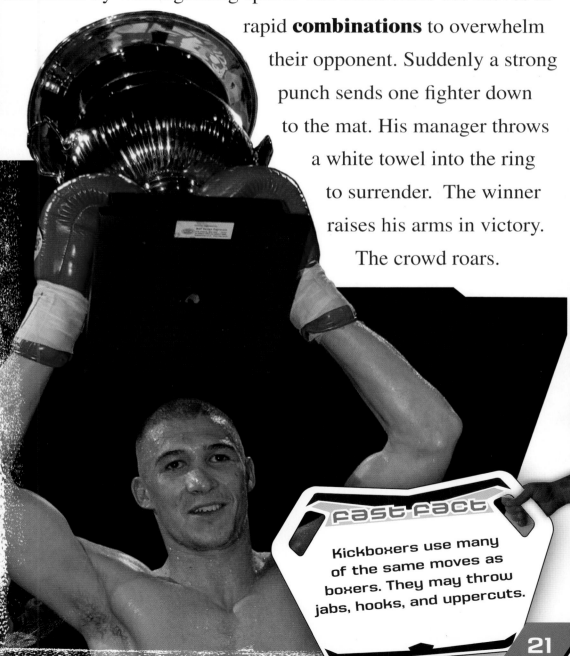

Most kickboxing matches start slow and end fast. The fighters test each other at first with light punches. They dance around the ring. In later rounds, punches are thrown and kicks fly with lightning speed. The kickboxers use moves in rapid **combinations** to overwhelm their opponent. Suddenly a strong punch sends one fighter down to the mat. His manager throws a white towel into the ring to surrender. The winner raises his arms in victory. The crowd roars.

Fast Fact

Kickboxers use many of the same moves as boxers. They may throw jabs, hooks, and uppercuts.

GLOSSARY

combinations—several moves done quickly in a row to overwhelm an opponent

headgear—a type of protective helmet made of leather or foam

karate—a kind of martial art focused on self-defense

knockout—fight outcome in which one fighter is knocked down by his or her opponent and cannot get up

martial art—a style of fighting and self-defense; for example, karate and judo are both martial arts.

opponents—people who fight against each other

round—a limited time period of fighting in a competitive match

spar—to practice kicks and punches with a partner without using full force

stamina—the energy and strength to do an activity for a long time

surrender—fight outcome in which one fighter gives up without having been knocked out

TO LEARN MORE

AT THE LIBRARY

Collins, Paul. *Muay Thai: Thai Boxing*.
Broomhall, Pa.: Chelsea, 2002.

Nonnemacher, Klaus. *Kickboxing*. Milwaukee,
Wisc.: Gareth Stevens, 2004.

Sievert, Terri. *Kickboxing*. Minneapolis, Minn.:
Capstone, 2004.

ON THE WEB

Learning more about kickboxing
is as easy as 1, 2, 3.

1. Go to www.factsurfer.com
2. Enter "kickboxing" into search box.
3. Click the "Surf" button and you will see a list
   of related web sites.

With factsurfer.com, finding more
information is just a click away.

INDEX